D1591119

PHILOSOPHY
AND LOGICAL SYNTAX

AMS PRESS

NEW YORK

PHILOSOPHY AND LOGICAL SYNTAX

BY

RUDOLF CARNAP

Professor of Philosophy in the German University of Prague

LONDON:
KEGAN PAUL, TRENCH, TRUBNER & Co. Ltd.
BROADWAY HOUSE CARTER LANE E.C.
1935

Library of Congress Cataloging in Publication Data

Carnap, Rudolf, 1891-1970.
  Philosophy and logical syntax.

  Reprint of the 1935 ed. published by K. Paul,
Trench, Trubner, London, which was issued as no. 70
of Psyche miniatures, general series.
  Bibliography: p.
  1. Logical positivism—Addresses, essays, lectures.
2. Logic, Symbolic and mathematical—Addresses,
essays, lectures.   3. Philosophy—Addresses, essays,
lectures.   I. Title.   II. Series: Psyche miniatures:
General series; no. 70.
B824.6.C28   1979   146'.4   75-41050
ISBN 0-404-14518-3

First AMS edition published in 1979.

Reprinted from the edition of 1935, London [Trim size has been
slightly altered in this edition. Original trim size: 10 x 15 cm. Text
area of the original has been maintained.

MANUFACTURED
IN THE UNITED STATES OF AMERICA

CONTENTS

5

PREFACE.

This book gives the content of three lectures delivered at the University of London in October, 1934. The first chapter has already been printed in *Psyche* (1934) ; and the present publication has been aided by a grant from the Publication Fund of the University of London, for which I desire to express my thanks.

My endeavour in these pages is to explain the main features of the *method of philosophising* which we, the Vienna Circle, use, and, by using try to develop further. It is the method of the logical analysis of science, or more precisely, of the *syntactical analysis of scientific language*. Only the method itself is here directly dealt with ; our special views, resulting from its use, appear rather in the form of examples (for instance our empiricist and anti-metaphysical position in the first chapter, our physicalist position in the last).

The purpose of the book—as of the lectures—is to give a first impression of our method and of the direction of our questions and investigations to those who are not yet acquainted with them. Therefore the form of presentation aims more at general lucidity that at scientific precision. Formulations which are more exact and therefore more suitable as a basis for argument, may be found in my book *Logische Syntax der Sprache*.

R. C.

Prague, November 1934.

PHILOSOPHY AND LOGICAL SYNTAX

I. THE REJECTION OF METAPHYSICS

1. *Verifiability*

The problems of philosophy as usually dealt with are of very different kinds. From the point of view which I am here taking we may distinguish mainly three kinds of problems and doctrines in traditional philosophy. For the sake of simplicity we shall call these parts *Metaphysics, Psychology*, and *Logic*. Or, rather, there are not three distinct regions, but three sorts of components which in most theses and questions are combined : a metaphysical, a psychological, and a logical component.

The considerations that follow belong to the third region : we are here carrying out *Logical Analysis*. The function of logical analysis is to analyse all knowledge, all assertions of science and of everyday life, in order to make clear the sense of each such assertion and the connections between them. One of the principal tasks of the logical analysis of a given proposition is to find out the method of verification for that proposition. The question is : What reasons can there be to assert this proposition ; or : How can we become certain as to its truth or falsehood ? This question is called by the philosophers the epistemological question ; epistemology or the philosophical theory of knowledge is nothing other than a special part of logical analysis, usually combined with some psychological questions concerning the process of knowing.

What, then, is the method of verification of a proposition? Here we have to distinguish between two kinds of verification : direct and indirect. If the question is about a proposition which asserts something about a present perception, *e.g.* " Now I see a red square on a blue ground," then the proposition can be tested directly by my present perception. If at present I do see a red square on a blue ground, the proposition is directly verified by this seeing ; if I do not see that, it is disproved. To be sure, there are still some serious problems in connection with direct verification. We will however not touch on them here, but give our attention to the question of *indirect* verification, which is more important for our purposes. A proposition P which is not directly verifiable can only be verified by direct verification of propositions deduced from P together with other already verified propositions.

Let us take the proposition P_1: " This key is made of iron." There are many ways of verifying this proposition; *e.g.*: I place the key near a magnet; then I perceive that the key is attracted. Here the deduction is made in this way:

Premises : P_1: " This key is made of iron;" the proposition to be examined.

P_2: " If an iron thing is placed near a magnet, it is attracted;" this is a physical law, already verified.

P_3: " This object—a bar—is a magnet;" proposition already verified.

P_4: " The key is placed near the bar;" this is now directly verified by our observation.

11

From these four premises we can deduce the conclusion :

P_5 : " The key will now be attracted by the bar."

This proposition is a prediction which can be examined by observation. If we look, we either observe the attraction or we do not. In the first case we have found a positive instance, an instance of verification of the proposition P_1 under consideration ; in the second case we have a negative instance, an instance of disproof of P_1.

In the first case the examination of the proposition P_1 is not finished. We may repeat the examination by means of a magnet, *i.e.* we may deduce other propositions similar to P_5 by the help of the same or similar premises as before. After that, or instead of that, we may make an examination by electrical tests, or by mechanical, chemical, or optical tests, etc. If in these further investigations all instances turn out to be positive, the certainty of the proposition P_1 gradually grows. We may soon come to a degree of certainty sufficient for all practical purposes, but *absolute* certainty we can never attain. The number of instances deducible from P_1 by the help of other propositions already verified or directly verifiable is *infinite*. Therefore there is always a possibility of finding in the future a negative instance, however small its probability may be. Thus the proposition P_1 *can never be completely verified*. For this reason it is called an *hypothesis*.

So far we have considered an individual proposition concerning one single thing. If we take a general proposition concerning all things or events at whatever time and place, a so-called natural *law*, it is still clearer that the number of examinable instances is infinite and so the proposition is an hypothesis.

Every assertion P in the wide field of science has this character, that it either asserts something about present perceptions or other experiences, and therefore is verifiable by them, or that propositions about future perceptions are deducible from P together with some other already verified propositions. If a scientist should venture to make an assertion from which no perceptive propositions could be deduced, what should we say to that? Suppose, *e.g.*, he asserts that there is not only a gravitational field having an effect on bodies according to the known laws of gravitation, but also a *levitational field*, and on being asked what sort of effect this levitational field has, according to his theory, he answers that there is no observable effect; in other words, he confesses his inability to give rules according to which we could deduce perceptive propositions from his assertion. In that case our reply is: your assertion is no assertion at all; it does not speak about anything; it is nothing but a series of empty words; it is simply without sense.

It is true that he may have images and even feelings connected with his words. This fact may be of psychological importance; logically, it is irrelevant. What gives theoretical meaning to a proposition is not the attendant images and thoughts, but the possibility of deducing from it perceptive propositions, in other words, the possibility of verification. To give sense to a proposition the presence of images is not sufficient; it is not even necessary. We have no actual image of the electro-magnetic field, nor even, I should say, of the gravitational field. Nevertheless the propositions which physicists assert about these fields have a perfect sense, because perceptive propositions are deducible from them. I by no means object to the proposition just mentioned about a levitational field that we do not know how to imagine or conceive such a field. My only objection to that proposition is that we are not told how to verify it.

2. *Metaphysics.*

What we have been doing so far is *logical analysis*. Now we are going to apply these considerations not to propositions of physics as before, but to propositions of *metaphysics*. Thus our investigation belongs to *logic*, to the third of the three parts of philosophy spoken about before, but the *objects* of this investigation belong to the first part.

I will call *metaphysical* all thosep ropositions which claim to represent knowledge about something which is over or beyond all experience, *e.g.* about the real Essence of things, about Things in themselves, the Absolute, and such like. I do not include in metaphysics those theories—sometimes called metaphysical—whose object is to arrange the most general propositions of the various regions of scientific knowledge in a well-ordered system; such theories belong actually to the field of empirical science, not of philosophy, however daring they may be. The sort of propositions I wish to denote as metaphysical may most easily be made clear by some examples: " The Essence and Principle of the world is Water," said Thales; " Fire," said Heraclitus; " the Infinite," said Anaximander; " Number," said Pythagoras. " All things are nothing but shadows of eternal ideas which themselves are in a spaceless and timeless sphere," is a doctrine of Plato. From the Monists we learn : " There is only one principle on which all that is, is founded "; but the Dualists tell us: " There are two principles." The Materialists say : " All that is, is in its essence material," but the Spiritualists say : " All that is, is spiritual." To metaphysics (in our sense of the word) belong the principal doctrines of Spinoza, Schelling, Hegel, and—to give at least one name of the present time— Bergson.

Now let us examine this kind of proposition from the point of view of *verifiability*. It is easy to realise that such propositions are not verifiable. From the proposition :

" The Principle of the world is Water "
we are not able to deduce any proposition
asserting any perceptions or feelings or
experiences whatever which may be ex-
pected for the future. Therefore the
proposition, " The Principle of the world
is Water," asserts nothing at all. It is
perfectly analogous to the proposition in
the fictive example above about the
levitational field and therefore it has no
more sense than that proposition. The
Water-Metaphysician—as we may call
him—has no doubt many images connected with his doctrine ; but they cannot
give sense to the proposition, any more
than they could in the case of the levitational field. Metaphysicians cannot
avoid making their propositions non-
verifiable, because if they made them
verifiable, the decision about the truth
or falsehood of their doctrines would
depend upon experience and therefore
belong to the region of empirical science.
This consequence they wish to avoid,
because they pretend to teach knowledge
which is of a higher level than that of
empirical science. Thus they are com-
pelled to cut all connection between their
propositions and experience ; and precisely

17

by this procedure they deprive them of any sense.

3. *Problems of Reality.*

So far I have considered only examples of such propositions as are usually called metaphysical. The judgment I have passed on these propositions, namely, that they have no empirical sense, may perhaps appear not very astonishing, and even trivial. But it is to be feared that the reader will experience somewhat more difficulty in agreement when I now proceed to apply that judgment also to philosophical doctrines of the type which is usually called epistemological. I prefer to call them also metaphysical because of their similarity, in the point under consideration, to the propositions usually so called. What I have in mind are the doctrines of Realism, Idealism, Solipsism, Positivism and the like, taken in their traditional form as asserting or denying the Reality of something. The Realist asserts the Reality of the external world, the Idealist denies it. The Realist— usually at least—asserts also the Reality of other minds, the Solipsist—an especially radical Idealist—denies it, and asserts that

18

only his own mind or consciousness is real. Have these assertions sense?

Perhaps it may be said that assertions about the reality or unreality of something occur also in empirical science, where they are examined in an empirical way, and that therefore they have sense. This is quite true. But we have to distinguish between two concepts of reality, one occurring in empirical propositions and the other occurring in the philosophical propositions just mentioned. When a zoologist asserts the reality of kangaroos, his assertion means that there are things of a certain sort which can be found and perceived at certain times and places; in other words that there are objects of a certain sort which are elements of the space-time-system of the physical world. This assertion is of course verifiable; by empirical investigation every zoologist arrives at a positive verification, independent of whether he is a Realist or an Idealist. Between the Realist and the Idealist there is full agreement as to the question of the reality of things of such and such sort, *i.e.* of the possibility of locating elements of such and such sort in the system of the physical world. The disagreement begins only when the question about the Reality of the physical world as a whole is raised. But this question has no sense, because the reality of anything is nothing else than the possibility of its being placed in a certain system, in this case, in the space-time-system of the physical world, and such a question has sense only if it concerns elements or parts, not if it concerns the system itself.

The same result is obtained by applying the criterion explained before: the possibility of deducing perceptive propositions. While from the assertion of the reality or the existence of kangaroos we *can* deduce perceptive propositions, from the assertion of the Reality of the physical world this is not possible; neither is it possible from the opposite assertion of the Unreality of the physical world. Therefore both assertions have no empirical content—no sense at all. It is to be emphasized that this criticism of having no sense applies equally to the assertion of Unreality. Sometimes the views of the *Vienna Circle* have been mistaken for a denial of the Reality of the physical world, but we make no such denial. It is true that we reject the thesis of the Reality of the physical world ; but we do not reject it as false, but as having no sense, and its Idealistic *anti*-thesis is subject to exactly the same rejection. We neither assert nor deny these theses, we reject the whole question.

All the considerations which apply to the question of the Reality of the physical world apply also to the other philosophical questions of Reality, *e.g.* the Reality of other minds, the Reality of the given, the Reality of universals, the Reality of qualities, the Reality of relations, the Reality of numbers, etc. If any philosophical thesis answering any of these questions positively or negatively is added to the system of scientific hypotheses, this system will not in the least become more effective; we shall not be able to make any further prediction as to future experiences. Thus all these philosophical theses are deprived of empirical content, of theoretical sense ; they are pseudo-theses.

If I am right in this assertion, the philosophical problems of Reality—as distinguished from the empirical problems of reality—have the same logical character as the problems (or rather, pseudo-problems) of transcendental metaphysics earlier referred to. For this reason I call those problems of Reality not epistemological problems—as they usually are called—but metaphysical.

Among the metaphysical doctrines that have no theoretical sense I have also mentioned *Positivism*, although the *Vienna Circle* is sometimes designated as Positivistic. It is doubtful whether this designation is quite suitable for us. In any case we do not assert the thesis that only the Given is Real, which is one of the principal theses of traditional Positivism. The name Logical Positivism seems more suitable, but this also can be misunderstood. At any rate it is important to realize that our doctrine is a logical one and has nothing to do with metaphysical theses of the Reality or Unreality of anything whatever. What the character of a *logical* thesis is, will be made clear in the following chapters.

4. *Ethics*.

One division of philosophy, which by some philosophers is considered the most important, has not been mentioned at all so far, namely, the philosophy of values, with its main branch, moral philosophy or *Ethics.* The word " Ethics " is used in two different senses. Sometimes a certain empirical investigation is called " Ethics," *viz.* psychological and sociological investigations about the actions of human beings, especially regarding the origin of these actions from feelings and volitions and their effects upon other people. Ethics in this sense is an empirical, scientific investigation ; it belongs to empirical science rather than to philosophy. Fundamentally different from this is ethics in the second sense, as the philosophy of moral values or moral norms, which one can designate normative ethics. This is not an investigation of facts, but a pretended investigation of what is good and what is evil, what it is right to do and what it is wrong to do. Thus the purpose of this philosophical, or normative, ethics is to state norms for human action or judgments about moral values.

It is easy to see that it is merely a difference of formulation, whether we state a norm or a value judgment. A norm or rule has an imperative form, for instance : " Do not kill ! " The corresponding value judgment would be : " Killing is evil." This difference of formulation has become practically very important, especially for the development of philosophical thinking. The rule, " Do not kill," has grammatically the imperative form and will therefore not be regarded as an assertion. But the value statement, " Killing is evil," although, like the rule, it is merely an expression of a certain wish, has the grammatical form of an assertive proposition. Most philosophers have been deceived by this form into thinking that a value statement is really an assertive proposition, and must be either true or false. Therefore they give reasons for their own value statements and try to disprove those of their opponents. But actually a value statement is nothing else than a command in a misleading grammatical form. It may have effects upon the actions of men, and these effects may either be in accordance with our wishes or not ; but it is neither true nor false. It does not assert anything and can neither be proved nor disproved.

This is revealed as soon as we apply to such statements our method of logical analysis. From the statement " Killing is evil " we cannot deduce any proposition about future experiences. Thus this statement is not verifiable and has no theoretical sense, and the same thing is true of all other value statements.

Perhaps somebody will contend in opposition that the following proposition is de-deducible: "If a person kills anybody he will have feelings of remorse." But this proposition is in no way deducible from the proposition "Killing is evil." It is deducible only from psychological propositions about the character and the emotional reactions of the person. These propositions are indeed verifiable and not without sense. They belong to psychology, not to philosophy ; to psychological ethics (if one wishes to use this word), not to philosophical or normative ethics. The propositions of normative ethics, whether they have the form of rules or the form of value statements, have no theoretical sense, are not scientific propositions (taking the word scientific to mean any assertive proposition).

To avoid misunderstanding it must be said that we do not at all deny the possibility and importance of a scientific investigation of value statements as well as of acts of valuation. Both of these are acts of individuals and are, like all other kinds of acts, possible objects of empirical investigation. Historians, psychologists, and sociologists may give analyses and causal explanations of them, and such historical and psychological propositions about acts of valuation and about value statements are indeed meaningful scientific propositions which belong to ethics in the first sense of this word. But the value statements themselves are here only objects of investigation ; they are not propositions in these theories, and have, here as elsewhere, no theoretical sense. Therefore we assign them to the realm of metaphysics.

5. *Metaphysics as Expression.*

Now we have analysed the propositions of metaphysics in a wide sense of this word, including not only transcendental metaphysics, but also the problems of philosophical Reality and lastly normative ethics. Perhaps many will agree that the propositions of all these kinds of metaphysics are not verifiable, *i.e.* that their truth cannot be examined by experience. And perhaps many will even grant that for this reason they have not the character of scientific propositions. But when I say that they are without sense, assent will probably seem more difficult. Someone may object : these propositions in the metaphysical books obviously have an effect upon the reader, and sometimes a very strong effect ; therefore they certainly *express* something. That is quite true, they *do* express something, but nevertheless they have no sense, no theoretical content.

We have here to distinguish two functions of language, which we may call the expressive function and the representative function. Almost all the conscious and unconscious movements of a person, including his linguistic utterances, express something of his feelings, his present mood, his temporary or permanent dispositions to reaction, and the like. Therefore we may take almost all his movements and words as symptoms from which we can infer something about his feelings or his character. That is the expressive function of movements and words. But besides that, a certain portion of linguistic utterances (*e.g.* " this book is black "), as distinguished from other linguistic utterances and movements, has a second function : these utterances represent a certain state of affairs ; they tell us that something is so and so ; they assert something, they predicate something, they judge something.

In special cases, this asserted state may be the same as that which is inferred from a certain expressive utterance ; but even in such cases we must sharply distinguish between the assertion and the expression. If, for instance, somebody is laughing, we may take this as a symptom of his merry mood ; if on the other hand he tells us without laughing : " Now I am merry," we can learn from his words the same thing which we inferred in the first case from his laughing. Nevertheless, there is a fundamental difference between the laughter and the words : " I am merry now." This linguistic utterance *asserts* the merry mood, and therefore it is either true or false. The laughter does not assert the merry mood but *expresses* it. It is neither true nor false, because it does not assert anything, although it may be either genuine or deceptive.

Now many linguistic utterances are analogous to laughing in that they have only an expressive function, no representative function. Examples of this are cries like " Oh, Oh " or, on a higher level, lyrical verses. The aim of a lyrical poem in which occur the words " sunshine " and " clouds," is not to inform us of certain meteorological facts, but to express certain feelings of the poet and to excite similar feelings in us. A lyrical poem has no assertional sense, no theoretical sense, it does not contain knowledge.

The meaning of our anti-metaphysical thesis may now be more clearly explained. This thesis asserts that metaphysical propositions — like lyrical verses—have only an expressive function, but no representative function. Metaphysical propositions are neither true nor false, because they assert nothing, they contain neither knowledge nor error, they lie completely outside the field of knowledge, of theory, outside the discussion of truth or falsehood. But they are, like laughing, lyrics, and music, expressive. They express not so much temporary feelings as permanent emotional or volitional dispositions. Thus, for instance, a Metaphysical system of Monism may be an expression of an even and harmonious mode of life, a Dualistic system may be an expression of the emotional state of someone who takes life as an eternal struggle ; an ethical system of Rigorism may be expressive of a strong sense of duty or perhaps of a desire to rule severely. Realism is often a symptom of the type of constitution called by psychologists extraverted, which is characterized by easily forming connections with men and things ; Idealism, of an opposite constitution, the so-called introverted type, which has a tendency to withdraw from the unfriendly world and to live within its own thoughts and fancies.

Thus we find a great similarity between metaphysics and lyrics. But there is one decisive difference between them. Both have no representative function, no theoretical content. A metaphysical proposition, however—as distinguished from a lyrical verse—*seems* to have some, and by this not only is the reader deceived, but the metaphysician himself. He believes that in his metaphysical treatise he has asserted something, and is led by this into argument and polemics against the propositions of some other metaphysician. A poet, however, does not assert that the verses of another are wrong or erroneous ; he usually contents himself with calling them bad.

The non-theoretical character of metaphysics would not be in itself a defect ; all arts have this non-theoretical character without thereby losing their high value for personal as well as for social life. The danger lies in the *deceptive* character of metaphysics ; it gives the illusion of knowledge without actually giving any knowledge. This is the reason why we reject it.

6. *Psychology.*

When we have eliminated metaphysical problems and doctrines from the region of knowledge or theory, there remain still two kinds of philosophical questions : psychological and logical. Now we shall eliminate the psychological questions also, not from the region of knowledge, but from philosophy. Then, finally, philosophy will be reduced to logic alone (in a wide sense of this word).

Psychological questions and propositions are certainly not without sense. From such propositions we can deduce other propositions about future experiences and

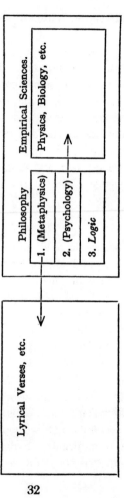

EXPRESSIVE FUNCTION
OF LANGUAGE.

Arts.

Lyrical Verses, etc.

REPRESENTATIVE FUNCTION
OF LANGUAGE.

Science (= the System of Theoretical Knowledge).

Philosophy

1. (Metaphysics)

2. (Psychology)

3. *Logic*

Empirical Sciences.

Physics, Biology, etc.

by their help we can verify the psychological propositions. But the propositions of psychology belong to the region of empirical science in just the same way as do the propositions of chemistry, biology, history and the like. The character of psychology is by no means more philosophical than that of the other sciences mentioned. When we look at the historical development of the sciences we see that philosophy has been the mother of them all. One science after another has been detached from philosophy and has become an independent science. Only in our time has the umbilical cord between psychology and philosophy been cut. Many philosophers have not yet realized quite clearly that psychology is no longer an embryo, but an independent organism, and that psychological questions have to be left to empirical research.

Of course we have no objection to connecting psychological and logical investigations, any more than to connecting investigations of any scientific kind. We reject only the confusion of the two kinds of questions. We demand that they should be clearly distinguished

B

even where in practice they are combined. The confusion sometimes consists in dealing with a logical question as if it were a psychological one. This mistake—called Psychologism—leads to the opinion that logic is a science concerning thinking, that is, either concerning the actual operation of thinking or the rules according to which thinking should proceed. But as a matter of fact the investigation of operations of thinking as they really occur is a task for psychology and has nothing to do with logic. And learning how to think *aright* is what we do in every other science as well as in logic. In astronomy we learn how to think aright about stars ; in logic we learn how to think aright about the special objects of logic. What these special objects of logic are, will be seen in the next chapter. In any case thinking is not an object of logic, but of psychology.

Psychological questions concern all kinds of so-called psychic or mental events, all kinds of sensations, feelings, thoughts, images, etc., whether they are conscious or unconscious. These questions of psychology can be answered only by experience, not by philosophising.

7. Logical Analysis.

The only proper **task** of *Philosophy* is *Logical Analysis*. And now the principal question to be answered here will be: "*What is logical analysis?*" In our considerations so far we have already practised logical analysis: we have tried to determine the character of physical hypotheses, of metaphysical propositions (or rather, pseudo-propositions), of psychological propositions. And now we have to apply logical analysis to logical analysis itself; we have to determine the character of the propositions of logic, of those propositions which are the results of logical analysis.

The opinion that metaphysical propositions have no sense because they do not concern any facts, has already been expressed by *Hume*. He writes in the last chapter of his "Enquiry Concerning Human Understanding" (published in the year 1748) as follows: "It seems to me, that the only objects of the abstract sciences or of demonstration, are quantity and number. . . . All other enquiries of men regard only matter of fact and existence; and these are evidently incapable of demonstration. . . . When we run over libraries, persuaded of these principles, what havoc must we make? If we take in our hand any volume, of divinity or school metaphysics, for instance; let us ask, Does it contain any abstract reasoning concerning quantity or number? No. Does it contain any experimental reasoning concerning matter of fact and existence? No. Commit it then to the flames: for it can contain nothing but sophistry and illusion." We agree with this view of Hume, which says—translated into our terminology—that only the propositions of mathematics and empirical science have sense, and that all other propositions are without sense.

But now it may perhaps be objected: "How about your own propositions? In consequence of your view your own writings, including this book, would be without sense, for they are neither mathematical nor empirical, that is, verifiable by experience." What answer can be given to this objection? What is the character of my propositions and in general of the propositions of logical analysis? This question is decisive for the consistency of the view which has been explained here.

An answer to the objection is given by Wittgenstein in his book *Tractatus Logico-Philosophicus*. This author has developed most radically the view that the propositions of metaphysics are shown by logical analysis to be without sense. How does he reply to the criticism that in that case his own propositions are also without sense? He replies by agreeing with it. He writes: " The result of philosophy is not a number of ' philosophical propositions,' but to make propositions clear " (p. 77). " My propositions are elucidatory in this way : he who understands me finally recognizes them as senseless, when he has climbed out through them, on them, over them. (He must so to speak throw away the ladder, after he has climbed up on it.) He must surmount these propositions ; then he sees the world rightly. Whereof one cannot speak, thereof one must be silent." (p. 189).

I, as well as my friends in the Vienna Circle, owe much to Wittgenstein, especially as to the analysis of metaphysics. But on the point just mentioned I cannot agree with him. In the first place he seems to me to be inconsistent in what he does. He tells us that one cannot state philosophical propositions and that whereof one cannot speak, thereof one must be silent ; and then instead of keeping silent, he writes a whole philosophical book. Secondly, I do not agree with his statement that all his propositions are quite as much without sense as metaphysical propositions are. My opinion is that a great number of his propositions (unfortunately not all of them) have in fact sense ; and that the same is true for all propositions of logical analysis.

It will be the purpose of the following chapters to give reasons for this positive answer to the question about the character of philosophical propositions, to show a way of formulating the results of logical analysis, a way not exposed to the objection mentioned, and thus to exhibit an *exact method of philosophy*.

II. LOGICAL SYNTAX OF LANGUAGE

1. *" Formal " Theory*

In this chapter an explanation will be given of a theory which we will call Logical Syntax, and it will be shown how to operate with the syntactical method. Although the word " philosophy " will not here occur, the syntactical method, as we shall try to make clear in the last chapter, brings us to the very basis of philosophy.

The logical syntax of a certain language is to be understood as the *formal* theory of that language. This needs further explanation. We will call "*formal* " such considerations or assertions concerning a linguistic expression as are without any reference to sense or meaning. A formal investigation of a certain sentence does not concern the sense of that sentence or the meaning of the single words, but only the kinds of words and the order in which they follow one another. Take, for instance the sentence : " The book is black."

If I assert that this expression consisting of four words is a sentence, and further, that the first word is an article, the second a substantive, the third a verb, and the fourth an adjective, all these assertions are formal assertions. If, however, I assert that that sentence concerns a book, or that its last word designates a colour, then my assertions are *not formal*, because they have to do with the *meaning* of the words. A formal investigation of a language would appear to have very narrow limits. Actually, however, this is not the case, because, as we shall see later, many questions and considerations which are expressed in a non-formal way can be formulated in the formal mode.

Such a formal theory of language is, so far as mathematics is concerned, already known by the work of *Hilbert*. Hilbert has propounded a theory, which he calls metamathematics or theory of proof, and in which the formal method is applied. In this theory of Hilbert, mathematics is dealt with as a system of certain symbols to be operated according to certain rules, and the meaning of the symbols is nowhere spoken of, but only the various kinds of symbols and the formal operations to which they are subjected. Now mathematics is a special part of the whole of language, which includes many other and quite different branches. And the same formal method which Hilbert has applied in his metamathematics to the system of mathematics, we apply in our logical syntax to the whole language-system of science, or to any special part of it, or to any other language-system whatsoever.

2. *Formation Rules*.

When we say that the objects of logical syntax are languages, the word " language " is to be understood as the *system of the rules* of speaking, as distinguished from the acts of speaking. Such a language-system consists of two kinds of rules, which we will call formation rules and transformation rules. The formation rules of a certain language-system *S* determine how *sentences* of the system *S* can be constructed out of the different kinds of symbols. One of the formation rules of the English language, for instance, determines that a series of four words, first an article, second a substantive, third a verb of a certain class, and fourth an adjective, constitutes a sentence. Such a formation rule is obviously similar to grammatical rules, especially to the rules of grammatical syntax. But the usual rules of grammatical syntax are not always strictly formal ; for instance, we may cite that rule of Latin grammar which determines that substantives designating women, countries, towns, or trees are of feminine gender. Such references to the meaning of the words are excluded in logical syntax as distinguished from grammatical syntax.

The totality of the formation rules of a language-system S is the same as the definition of the term " sentence of S." This definition can be stated in the following form : " A series of words is then, and only then, a sentence of the system S, if it has either this, that, or the other form." Now for a natural language, such as English, the formation rules can scarcely be given completely ; they are too complicated. The logicians, as we know, have made language-systems—or at least frameworks for such—which are much simpler and also much more exact than the natural languages. Instead of words, they use symbols similar to the mathematical symbols. Take, for example, the most developed of these symbolic languages, that constructed by Whitehead and Russell in their work *Principia Mathematica*. Two of the principal formation rules of this language are as follows : (1) an expression consisting of a predicate (that is, one of the small Greek letters 'ϕ', 'ψ', etc.) and one or more individual variables (the small Roman letters 'x', 'y', etc.) is a sentence ; (2) an expression consisting of two sentences and one connecting sign ('v', '$.$', '$\supset$', '$\equiv$') between them is also a sentence.

3. *Transformation Rules.*

Much more important than the formation rules are the transformation rules. They determine how given sentences may be transformed into others ; in other words : how from given sentences we may *infer* others. Thus in the English language there is the rule, that from the two sentences :

	" all a are b "
and	" all b are c "

we may infer : " all a are c."

Here only the framework of the sentences is given, not the sentences themselves. In order to make sentences we

43

have to substitute three English substantives in the plural form for the three letters 'a,' 'b,' 'c.' To give an illustration, from the two sentences :

| | " all eagles are birds " |
| and | " all birds are beasts " |

we may infer : " all eagles are beasts."

In the symbolic language of Whitehead and Russell we have the following rule : from two sentences of the form

| | " A " |
| and | " A$\supset$B ", where '$\supset$' is the implication-sign |

we may infer : " B ".

The totality of the transformation rules of a language-system S may be formulated as the definition of the term " *direct consequence* in S." Thus the transformation rules of the Principia Mathematica may be stated as follows : " In the system PM a sentence is to be called a direct consequence of a class of other sentences —called premises—then and only then, if one of the following conditions is fulfilled :

(1) the sentence has the form ' B ' and the class of premises consists of ' A ' and ' A$\supset$B ';

(2) ...;

(3) ... "

It is to be noted that an axiom or primitive sentence of a language can also be stated in the form of a rule of inference, and therefore also in the form of a part of the definition of " direct consequence." The difference is only that in this case the class of premises is the null class (*i.e.* the class which has no members). Thus instead of ruling: " ' p⊃.pvq ' is to be a primitive sentence of the language S ", we may say: " ' p⊃.pvq ' is to be a direct consequence of the null class of premises." If a class P of premises is connected with a certain sentence C by a chain of sentences in such a way that every sentence of this chain is a direct consequence of some sentences preceding in the chain, we call the sentence C a *consequence* of the class P of premises. This term " consequence " is, as we shall soon see, one of the most important terms of logical syntax.

We have seen that a language-system is a system of rules of formation and transformation. According to this the logical syntax of a language-system S consists of two parts: the investigation or analysis of the formation rules of S, and that of the transformation rules of S. The first part is, as observed above, somewhat similar to grammar, the second part, to logic, especially to the logic of inference or deduction. It is generally supposed that grammar and logic have quite different characters, grammar being concerned with linguistic expressions, and logic with the *meaning* of thoughts or of propositions. But in opposition to this the development of modern logic has shown more and more clearly that the rules of inference *can* be expressed in a purely *formal* manner, that is, without any reference to meaning. Our task is merely to draw the consequence from this development and to construct the whole system of logic in a strictly formal way. We shall then have to do neither with thoughts as mental acts nor with their contents, but only with sentences, and with sentences not as vehicles of meaning or sense, but only as series of symbols, of written, spoken, or other signs. It will now be clear why we do not employ here the usual word " proposition." Sometimes it means, not a sentence, but what is expressed by a sentence, and very often it is used ambiguously. Therefore we prefer to use the word " sentence."

Between logic and grammar, or in other words, between the transformation rules and the formation rules, there is no fundamental difference. Transformation or inference depends only upon the formal character of the sentences, only upon their syntactical form. That is the reason why we apply the name " syntax " not, as is usually done in linguistics, to the formation rules alone, but to the system containing both kinds of rules together.

4. *Syntactical Terms*.

The terms " sentence " and " direct consequence " are the two primitive terms of logical syntax—or " syntax," as we may briefly call it where there is no danger of misunderstanding. Every other term of syntax can be defined on the basis of these two terms. We will now give the definitions of several syntactical terms which are among the most important, especially, as we shall see later, in the application to philosophical questions.

Given any language-system, or set of formation rules and transformation rules, among the sentences of this language there will be true and false sentences. But we cannot define the terms " true " and

" false " in syntax, because whether a given sentence is true or false will generally depend not only upon the syntactical form of the sentence, but also upon experience ; that is to say, upon something extra-linguistic. It may be however that in certain cases a sentence is true or false only by reason of the rules of the language. Such sentences we will call *valid* and *contravalid* respectively.

Our definition of validity is as follows : a sentence is called *valid*, if it is a consequence of the null class of premises. Thus in the language of Russell the sentence ' pv ∼ p '—usually called the Principle of the Excluded Middle—is a valid sentence ; and so likewise are all other sentences for which proofs are given in the *Principia Mathematica*. A proof in this work is a series of sentences of such kind that each sentence of the series is either a primitive sentence or inferred from preceding sentences of the series. Now a primitive sentence is a direct consequence of the null class of premises. Therefore a proof in the *Principia Mathematica* is a chain of direct consequences beginning with the null class of premises and ending with the sentence proved.

This proved sentence is thus a consequence of the null class and therefore—according to our definition—valid.

Turning to the term "contravalid": a sentence 'A' of a certain language-system is called *contravalid* if every sentence of this system is a consequence of 'A.' Every sentence of the language of Principia Mathematica which can be disproved in this system (*e.g.* "p.∼p" and "∼(p≡p"), is contravalid. Disproving a sentence 'A' consists in showing that a certain sentence 'B' as well as '∼B', the negation of 'B', are consequences of 'A'. But from two mutually opposed sentences such as 'B' and '∼B' any sentence whatever can be deduced. Therefore, if 'B' and '∼B' are consequences of 'A', every sentence is a consequence of 'A,' and 'A' is contravalid.

We will call a sentence *determinate* if it is either valid or contravalid. We will call a sentence *indeterminate* if it is neither valid nor contravalid. Thus the determinate sentences are those whose truth-value is determined by the rules of the language. In the language-system of Russell one may construct *in*determinate sentences by introducing *non*-logical

49

constants. Suppose, for instance, 'a' and 'b' to be names of persons, 'S' to designate the relation of sonship, then 'aSb' (in words : " a is a son of b ") is an indeterminate sentence, because its truth can obviously not be determined by the rules of the system of Russell.

5. *L-Terms*.

In the symbolic languages of modern logic the transformation rules, to which, as has been pointed out above, the primitive sentences also belong, are usually chosen in such a way that they seem to be right for logical or mathematical reasons. But it would likewise be possible to state a language-system which, besides such logical rules, also contained extra-logical ones. Take for instance the system of *Principia Mathematica*. In its present form it contains only such primitive sentences and rules of inference as have a purely logical character. Transformation rules of this logical or mathematical character we will call *L-rules*. Now we could add to the system of *Principia Mathematica* transformation rules of an extra-logical character, for instance some physical laws as primitive sentences, as, for example, Newton's principles of mechanics, Maxwell's equations of electromagnetics, the two principles of thermodynamics, and such like. In order to have a comprehensive name for the extralogical transformation rules we will call them physical rules or *P-rules*.

Thus a transformation rule of a language is either an L-rule or a P-rule. The distinction of these two kinds of rules is very important. We have only given some rough indications of it, but it is possible to define this distinction in an exact and strictly formal way, that is, without any reference to the sense of the sentences. Omitting this exact definition for the sake of brevity, however, let us simply suppose that there is given a certain language-system, for instance the system of Principia Mathematica with the addition of some physical laws as primitive sentences, in which the given transformation rules are already divided into L-rules and P-rules.

We have called a sentence C a *consequence* of a class P of sentences—the premises—if there is a chain of sentences constructed according to the transformation rules connecting the class P with the sentence C. Suppose now that in a certain case only L-rules are applied ; then we call C an *L-consequence* of P. If on the other hand C can be deduced from P only by applying also P-rules, in other words if C is a consequence, but not an L-consequence, of P, we call C a *P-consequence* of P. Let us take for example the following class P of two premises :

P_1 : The body A has a mass of 3 grammes.

P_2 : The body B has a mass of 6 grammes.

Then we can deduce from P the following two consequences among others :

C_1 : The mass of B is double the mass of A.

C_2 : If the same force is acting on A and on B, the acceleration of A will be double that of B.

For the deduction of C_1 we need only L-rules, that is rules of logic and arithmetic, while for the deduction of C_2 besides these we need P-rules, namely the laws of mechanics. Therefore C_1 is an L-consequence, but C_2, a P-consequence, of the class P of premises.

As we have defined corresponding to the term " consequence " an L-term and a P-term, we may in an analogous way define corresponding L-terms and P-terms for the other general terms already defined. Thus we will call a sentence which is true by reason of the L-rules alone, L-valid or *analytic*. The exact definition of this term is perfectly analogous to the definition of " valid " : a sentence is called analytic if it is an L-consequence of the null class of premises. Similarly we will call a sentence which is false by reason of the L-rules alone, L-contravalid or *contradictory*. The formal definition is as follows : a sentence is called contradictory if every sentence of the language is an L-consequence of the same. A sentence is called *L-determinate* if it is either analytic or contradictory. If for the determination of the truth or falsehood of a given sentence the L-rules do not suffice, in other words if the sentence is not L-determinate, it is called L-indeterminate or *synthetic*. The synthetic sentences are those which assert states of affairs. The terms " analytic " and " synthetic " have already been used in traditional philosophy ; they are especially important in the philosophy of Kant; but up till now they have not been exactly defined.

In a language-system which contains only L-rules, for instance in the system of *Principia Mathematica*, each of the defined general terms agrees completely with the corresponding L-term. Thus every valid sentence (for instance ' $p \lor \sim p$ ') is analytic, every contravalid sentence (for instance ' $p . \sim p$ ') is contradictory; indeterminate sentences, and only these (for instance ' aSb,' " a is a son of b "), are synthetic.

General terms	L-terms	P-terms
consequence valid contravalid	L-consequence (L-valid) *analytic* (L-contravalid) *contradictory*	P-consequence P-valid P-contravalid
determinate indeterminate	L-determinate (L-indeterminate) *synthetic*	
content equipollent synonymous		

If a sentence is valid, but not analytic, we call it *P-valid*. If a sentence is contravalid, but not contradictory, we call it *P-contravalid*. The other P-terms are not so important.

54

The terms just defined give a classification of sentences which we may represent by the following scheme :

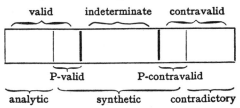

The totality of the sentences of the language is comprehended in the above diagram. Some of the sentences are either valid or contravalid, according to the transformation rules in general ; the others are indeterminate. Among the valid sentences some are analytic, namely those which are valid on the basis of the L-rules alone ; the others are P-valid. In the same way some of the contravalid sentences are contradictory, the others P-contravalid. The sentences which are neither analytic nor contradictory are synthetic. The three L-terms, namely " analytic," " synthetic " and " contradictory," are very often used in the logical analysis of any scientific theory. Later on we shall consider some examples.

6. *Content.*

If we wish to characterize the purport of a given sentence, its contents, its assertive power, so to speak, we have to regard the class of those sentences which are consequences of the given sentence. Among these consequences we may leave aside the valid sentences, because they are consequences of every sentence. We define therefore as follows : the class of the non-valid consequences of a given sentence is called the *content* of this sentence.

The method which we are using here and which we call logical syntax is characterized by limiting itself to terms defined in a strictly formal way. One might perhaps be inclined to think that it is a defect of this formal method not to be able to deal with questions of *sense*. But in fact this method *is* able to do that, at least in a certain respect. Concerning a given series of signs, for instance a series of words in a word-language, there are *two* questions of sense. The first is, whether that series of words *has* a sense or not. If here " sense " means " theoretical sense," " assertive sense," then such a question can be answered within the range of *formal* investigation, namely by the help of the formal, syntactical term " sentence " defined by the formation rules of the language. Secondly it may be asked *what* sense a given sentence has. This question can be answered by the help of the formal, syntactical term " content " as just defined.

The content of a sentence represents its sense, so far as the word " sense " is intended to designate something of a purely *logical* character. Sometimes by " sense " is meant the kind of thoughts and images that are connected with the given sentence. But in this case the question is a psychological one and has to be examined by the experimental method of psychology. In logical analysis we are not concerned with such questions. All questions of sense having an actually logical character can be dealt with by the formal method of syntax.

Sometimes two sentences of quite unlike wording nevertheless have the same sense, as asserting the same state. We will call such sentences *equipollent*. The formal definition is obvious : two sentences are called equipollent if they have the same content, in other words if they are consequences of each other. Similarly two expressions which are not themselves sentences, but occur in sentences, may have the same sense, the same meaning, in spite of a quite different wording. This relation, which we will designate by the term "*synonymous*," can also be defined in a formal manner : two expressions are called mutually synonymous, if the content of any sentence containing one of them is not changed if we replace that expression by the other. Thus, for instance, the expressions ' 5 + 2 ' and ' 4 + 3 ' are synonymous, because the content of a sentence will not be changed if we replace in this sentence ' 5 + 2 ' by ' 4 + 3 ' or *vice versa*.

7. *Pseudo-Object-Sentences.*

The above are some examples of syntactical terms, all based upon the term " consequence " which is the principal term of syntax. The task of syntax is to state such definitions as those of the given examples and to analyze given sentences, proofs, theories, and the like, by the help of such syntactical terms. The results of such an analysis are then formulated as *syntactical sentences* having for instance the following form : " Such and such a sentence contained in a certain theory is synthetic, but a certain other sentence is merely analytic," or : " This particular word of such a theory is synonymous, but not L-synonymous, with that and that combination of words," and so on.

If sentences of this simple form containing well-defined syntactical terms are given, it is easy to see that they are syntactical sentences. But there are other sentences which *seem* to be of quite a different kind and nevertheless really are syntactical. This fact is very important, especially in dealing with philosophical sentences. I have already mentioned **my** opinion, which will be explained in the next chapter, that philosophical sentences belong to syntax. It must be confessed that this opinion seems not to agree with obvious facts, for philosophical sentences—even after the elimination of metaphysics—seem to concern not only the form of linguistic expressions but also, and perhaps mainly, quite other objects, such as the structure of space and time, the relation between cause and effect, the relation between things and their qualities, the difference and the real relations between the physical and the psychical, the character of numbers and numerical functions, the necessity, contingency, possibility or impossibility of conditions, and the like. We shall have to show later that philosophical sentences of such kinds only *seem* by their deceptive appearance to concern the objects mentioned, but that they really concern linguistic forms. For the present, however, we shall not enter into the consideration of such philosophical sentences, but will try to explain in general under what conditions a sentence has such a deceptive form.

For this purpose we will distinguish three kinds of sentences. About *syntactical sentences* I have just spoken; they concern the form of linguistic expressions. With these are to be contrasted those sentences which concern not linguistic expressions but extra-linguistic objects; they may be called *real object-sentences*. There is also a third, an intermediate kind of sentence. Sentences of this kind are, so to speak, amphibious, being like object-sentences as to their form, but like syntactical sentences as to their contents. They may be called *seudo - object - sentences*.

60

1. Real object-sentences. (Empirical Science)	2. Pseudo-object-sentences. Material mode of speech. (Philo		3. Syntactical sentences. Formal mode of speech. sophy)
1a. The rose is red.	1b. The rose is a thing. Q_1 (a)	1c.	The word 'rose' is a thing-word. Q_2 ('a')
	2b. The first lecture treated of metaphysics.	2c.	The first lecture contained the word 'metaphysics.'
3a. Mr. A visited Africa.	3b. This book treats of Africa.	3c.	This book contains the word 'Africa.'
4a. The evening-star and the earth are about equal in size.	4b. The evening-star and the morning-star are identical.	4c.	The words 'evening-star' and 'morning-star' are synonymous.

Let us look at the examples tabulated on the opposite page. (1a) "The rose is red" is a real object-sentence which concerns the rose as object. (1c) "The word ' rose ' is a thing-word" is a syntactical sentence ; its object is not the thing rose but the word ' rose,' a linguistic expression. Finally (1b) "The rose is a thing" is an example of a *pseudo*-object-sentence. This sentence has the same grammatical subject as the sentence 1a and thus appears, like it, to concern the thing, rose, but there is a fundamental difference between the two sentences. The sentence 1a is synthetic ; it really asserts some quality of the rose. But from the sentence 1b we cannot learn any quality of the rose, neither as to its colour, nor size, nor form, nor anything else. This sentence 1b is analytic ; we can ascertain its truth without observing any rose, by only considering to what syntactical kind the word ' rose ' belongs, namely that it is a thing-word. Thus we see that the sentence 1b asserts the same as 1c, because always and only when a certain object is a thing is its designating word a thing-word.

We may call the quality of being a thing-designation a *parallel syntactical quality* to the quality of being a thing. The **general** definition will be: a syntactical quality Q_2 is called *parallel* to the quality Q_1 if it is the case that when, and only when, an object possesses the quality Q_1 does a designation of this object possess the quality Q_2. And the criterion of a pseudo-object-sentence can now be stated as follows (if we regard only sentences of the simplest form) : such a sentence attributes to an object (say **a**) a quality Q_1 to which a parallel syntactical quality Q_2 can be found. Such a sentence ' Q_1(a) ' can then be translated into the syntactical sentence ' Q_2(' a ') ' which attributes the quality Q_2 to a designation of that object.

This brings out more clearly the difference between the sentences 1a and 1b. While to the quality of being a thing there is a parallel syntactical quality, namely that of being a thing-designation, to the quality of being red there is *no* parallel syntactical quality—the designations of red things have no common characteristic syntactical quality. For instance, from the designation " my pencil " alone we are not able to decide whether it is a designation of a red thing or not ; we should have to look at the designated object itself, namely my pencil. Therefore the sentence " The rose is red " is *not* a *pseudo*-object-sentence, but a *real* object sentence.

8. *The Material and the Formal Modes of Speech.*

All sentences of empirical science, all sentences asserting facts, whether they are general or individual, are real object-sentences. All sentences of logical analysis on the other hand, and—as we shall see in the next chapter—of philosophy, belong to the second or to the third kind. Thus in our further considerations, these two kinds of sentences are chiefly considered. They differ, as we have seen, not so much in their purport or contents as in their formulation. In the mode of speech applied in pseudo-object-sentences there are used words which designate objects or matter, while the words used in syntactical sentences obviously concern form. For this reason we shall call the pseudo-object-sentences also sentences of the *material mode of speech*, while we shall assign the syntactical sentences to the *formal mode of speech*.

The difference between these two modes of speech may be made clearer by a few examples. Take the sentence: "The first chapter treats of metaphysics." This sentence belongs to the material mode; the corresponding sentence of the formal mode is: "The first chapter contains the word 'metaphysics'." To take a more striking example, suppose we have a geographical book about Africa and we make the statement: "This book treats of Africa." Then this sentence (3b) belongs to the material mode; the corresponding sentence of the formal mode is: "This book contains the word 'Africa'" (3c). The sentence 3b is in its form analogous to the sentence "Mr. A visited Africa" (3a); but there is a principal difference between the two sentences. The sentence 3a asserts something about Africa. The sentence 3b—being analogous —*seems* to assert something about Africa, but really *does not*. It is not a quality of Africa to be treated of in that book, because one might know everything about Africa and nevertheless nothing about that book. It is only a quality of the word 'Africa' to be contained in the book. On the other hand, it is really a quality of Africa to be visited by Mr. A. Here we see the deceptive character of the material mode ; the sentences of this mode seem to concern something which they in fact do not concern.

As an example of a somewhat different kind let us examine sentence 4b : " The evening-star and the morning-star are identical," or " . . . are the same thing." This sentence is in its form analogous to sentence 4a : " The evening-star and the earth are about equal in size " ; but 4b is in fact a pseudo-object sentence which is to be translated into the following syntactical sentence (4c) : " The words ' evening-star ' and ' morning-star ' are synonymous." The sentence 4a asserts that there is a certain relation between two certain objects. The sentence 4b *seems* to do the same, but it is obvious that it really does not. There cannot be *two* objects concerned here, because the two names designate only one object, namely a particular planet. But not even this object is concerned in the sentence 4b, for it is easy to see that it does not assert any quality whatever of that planet. It asserts only something about the two designations, namely that they designate the same thing, or, expressed in syntactical terms, that they are synonymous.

Here we find again that deceptive character of the material mode as to the subject-matter of its sentences. Most of the sentences of *philosophy* deceive us in this way, because, as we shall see, most of them are formulated in the material mode of speech.

III. SYNTAX AS THE METHOD
OF PHILOSOPHY

1. *The Material Mode of Speech.*

In the first chapter I tried to explain
why I reject metaphysics and why I
believe that the task of philosophy is
logical analysis. The principal question
that we have now to answer is : What is
logical analysis ? What kind of sentences
are those that express the results of logical
analysis ? My answer—as I have already
indicated—will be that they are syntactical
sentences, sentences of logical syntax, and
that philosophy is thus the application
of the syntactical method.

In the last chapter we discovered that
the number of sentences which belong to
syntax is much greater than it seems to
be at first glance, because many sentences
which are really syntactical have a deceptive form, a form which makes us mistake
them for object-sentences. Sentences of
such a form we have called pseudo-object-
sentences or sentences of the *material mode*

of speech. We have seen how they can be translated into the formal mode of speech, that is, into sentences manifestly belonging to syntax. These considerations will be of special importance for such sentences as express results of logical analysis, because those sentences are, as will be shown, very often, and perhaps for the most part, expressed in the material mode of speech. The use of this material mode often leads to confusion and idle philosophical controversies which can be settled by translating the theses of the controversy into the formal mode.

Let us begin with some examples already mentioned. The sentence, " The rose is a thing," belongs to the material mode. It can be translated into the following sentence of the formal mode : " The word ' rose ' is a thing-designation." In general every sentence of the form " Such and such is a *thing* " belongs to the material mode. There are many other words which function in the same way as the word ' thing,' for instance the words ' quality,' ' relation,' ' number,' ' event.' Thus the statement, " Friendship is not a quality but a relation," is a sentence of the material mode which can be translated into the formal mode as : " The word ' friendship ' is not a quality-designation but a relation-designation " By this translation it becomes clear that it is the *word* ' friendship ' which is here concerned, and not friendship itself, as is falsely suggested by the form of the original sentence. To take another example, this time arising out of the logical analysis of the notion of number, the sentence " 7 is not a thing but a number," is merely the expression in the material mode of the formal sentence, " The sign ' 7 ' is not a thing-sign but a numerical sign."

Hence it is apparent that if we wish to avoid the dangerous material mode, we must avoid the word ' thing ' and use instead the parallel syntactical term ' thing-designation ' ; analogously, instead of the word ' number ' we have to use the term ' numerical designation,' instead of ' quality,' ' quality-designation,' instead of ' relation,' ' relation-designation,' instead of ' event,' ' event-designation,' instead of ' space,' ' spatial designation ' or ' spatial co-ordinates,' instead of ' time,' ' time-designation ' or ' time-co-ordinates,' and so on. It will be easily seen without further examples that in this way many results of logical analysis turn out in fact to be syntactical.

In the last chapter we showed that the sentence " This book treats of Africa," was a sentence of the material mode, capable of being translated into the formal statement, " This book contains the word ' Africa '." Similarly, to the material mode belong all those sentences which assert that a certain sentence or treatise or theory or science *deals with* such and such objects, or *describes* or *asserts* such and such facts or states or events ; or that a certain word or expression *designates* or *signifies* or *means* such and such an object.

Among such sentences dealing with the purport, meaning, or signification of something, especially important are those which express the result of the comparison of two theses or two theories or the like, and assert that both have the same purport or meaning, or that both express the same facts or states. For the translation of such sentences into the formal mode we make use of the syntactical term ' equipollent ' as defined above, and the assertion becomes : "Those theses, theories, etc. are *equipollent*." Analogously, sentences such as " These expressions have the same signification " or " . . . designate the same object " are translated (according to our definition of the term ' synonymous ') into the form : " These expressions are *synonymous*."

By this method of translation into the formal mode we free logical analysis from all reference to the extra-linguistic objects themselves, and we are then concerned merely with the form of linguistic expressions. It is perhaps hardly necessary to emphasize the fact that this conclusion applies only to *logical analysis*, and that there is no question of eliminating reference to objects themselves from *object-sciences*. On the contrary, these sciences are really concerned with objects themselves, with things, not merely with thing-designations.

2. *Modalities*.

Now let us consider some terms of a quite different kind, the so-called *Modalities*, namely, possibility, impossibility, necessity and contingency. These ideas have at all times greatly exercised the minds of philosophers. Recently the logic of modalities has been treated with greater exactitude by means of the construction of axiomatic systems in which the modalities are given as principal concepts. But we find that the authors of these systems discuss certain questions (for instance that of the true meaning of possibility) for which there is given neither an unambiguous answer nor a method of resolution. In my opinion this is a symptom that in these systems the logical character of the modalities is not conceived with complete clarity.

Modality sentences are in fact veiled syntactical sentences, namely sentences of the material mode of speech. To what do we usually apply modalities, for instance, possibility or impossibility? We apply them to conditions, states, events, and such like—to take an example, " That A is older than B, and B is older than A, is an impossible state." This sentence can be translated from the material into the formal mode in the following way : ' The sentence ' A is older than B, and B is older than A ' is contradictory." That the term ' impossible ' belongs in fact to the material mode, may be easily shown by the criterion previously explained : Impossibility is a quality to which there is a parallel syntactical quality, namely contradictoriness, because

73   D

always and only when a state is impossible, is the sentence which describes this state contradictory, as, for instance, in the example given.

Sometimes, however, the idea of impossibility has the sense not of *logical*, but of *physical* or *real* impossibility. In this latter case the parallel syntactical term is not ' contradictory ' but the corresponding general term, namely ' *contravalid*.' Take for instance the sentence, " The state of a particular solid iron ball swimming on the water is physically impossible." The translation is : " The sentence ' This solid iron ball is swimming on the water ' is contravalid." Here the sentence is in fact P-contravalid, that is, incompatible with the system of physical laws.

The other modality-terms belong likewise to the material mode. As possibility is the opposite of impossibility, obviously the parallel syntactical term to ' logically possible ' is ' non-contradictory,' and the parallel syntactical term to ' physically possible ' is ' non-contravalid.' Analogously, we translate ' logically necessary ' into ' analytic,' and ' physically necessary ' into ' valid.' For instance, instead of

saying in the material mode : " That an
iron ball is heavier than a wooden ball
of equal size, is physically necessary," we
say in the formal mode : " The sentence
' An iron ball is heavier than a wooden
ball of equal size ' is valid." In this case
the sentence is P-valid, that is, logically
deducible from the system of physical
laws. Finally we have the modality term
' contingent ' (in the sense of ' neither
necessary nor impossible '). We translate
' logically contingent ' into ' synthetic,'
and ' physically contingent ' into ' indeterminate.'

Modality terms	Parallel syntactical terms	
	L-terms	General terms
log. or phys. impossible	contradictory	contravalid
log. or phys. possible	non-contradictory	non-contravalid
log. or phys. necessary	analytic	valid
log. or phys. contingent	synthetic	indeterminate

3. *Relativity in Regard to Language.*

Now it may be asked why I repeatedly
propose to translate sentences which are
formulated in the material mode of speech

into the formal mode. I do this for the purpose of showing that such sentences belong to the field of syntax. By the application of the material mode this character of the sentences is disguised ; we are deceived—as we have seen—as to their real subject-matter. But there are still greater disadvantages of the material mode. It involves the danger of getting into useless philosophical controversies.

To take a case in point, in the different systems of modern arithmetic dealt with logically, numbers are given different status. For instance in the system of Whitehead and Russell numbers are treated as classes of classes, while in the systems of Peano and of Hilbert they are taken as primitive objects. Suppose two philosophers get into a dispute, one of them asserting : " Numbers are classes of classes," and the other : " No, numbers are primitive objects, independent elements." They may philosophize without end about the question what numbers really are, but in this way they will never come to an agreement. Now let them both translate their theses into the formal mode. Then the first philosopher makes the assertion : " Numerical expressions

are class-expressions of the second order ";
and the other says : " Numerical expressions are not class-expressions, but elementary expressions."

In this form, however, the two sentences are not yet quite complete. They
are syntactical sentences concerning certain linguistic expressions. But a syntactical sentence must refer to one or
several specific language-systems ; it is
incomplete unless it contains such a
reference. If the language-system of
Peano is called L_1, and that of Russell L_2,
the two sentences may be completed as
follows : " In L_1 numerical expressions
are elementary expressions," and : " In
L_2 numerical expressions are class expressions of the second order." Now these
assertions are compatible with each other
and both are true ; the controversy has
ceased to exist.

Very often sterile philosophical controversies arise through such an incompleteness of theses. This incompleteness is
concealed by the usual formulation in the
material mode. When translated into
the formal mode, the want of reference
to language is noticed at once. Then by
adding such a reference the theses are

made complete, and thereby the controversy becomes clear and exact. Even then it will sometimes still be difficult to decide which side is right ; but sometimes it is as simple as in the example just considered, and the dispute obviously vanishes. *The relativity of all philosophical theses in regard to language*, that is, the need of reference to one or several particular language-systems, is a very essential point to keep in mind. It is on account of the general use of the material mode of speech that this relativity is nearly always left unnoticed.

4. *Pseudo-questions.*

In the example mentioned the theses are only incomplete ; they can easily be translated into the formal mode and completed, and thus they become precise. In other cases, however, the use of the material mode leads to metaphysical pseudo-theses which cannot be so easily corrected. I do not mean that the sentences of the material mode are themselves necessarily pseudo-theses or without sense, but only that they often mislead us into stating other sentences or questions which are so. For instance, in the material mode we speak about numbers instead of numerical expressions. That is not in itself bad or incorrect, but it leads us into the temptation to raise questions as to the real essence of numbers, such as the philosophical questions whether numbers are real objects or ideal objects, whether they are extramental or intramental, whether they are objects-in-themselves or merely intentional objects of thinking, and the like. I do not know how such questions could be translated into the formal mode or into any other unambiguous and clear mode ; and I doubt whether the philosophers themselves who are dealing with them are able to give us any such precise formulation. Therefore it seems to me that these questions are metaphysical pseudo-questions.

If we use the formal mode of speech, we are not speaking about numbers, but about numerical expressions. We can then raise many questions concerning the syntactical character of the numerical expressions in a certain system or in different systems, but we do not arrive at pseudo-questions of the kind mentioned. Against these we are protected automatically, so to speak, by the use of the formal mode.

What are the practical consequences of these considerations as to the formulation of philosophical theses? There is no need to eliminate completely the material mode of speech. This mode is usual and perhaps sometimes suitable. But it must be handled with special caution. In all decisive points of discussion it is advisable to replace the material by the formal mode; and in using the formal mode, reference to the language-system must not be neglected. It is not necessary that the thesis should refer to a language-system already put forward; it may sometimes be desired to formulate a thesis on the basis of a so far unknown language-system, which is to be characterized by just this thesis. In such a case the thesis is not an assertion, but a proposal or project, in other words a part of the definition of the designed language-system.

If one partner in a philosophical discussion cannot or will not give a translation of his thesis into the formal mode, or if he will not state to which language-system his thesis refers, then the other will be well-advised to refuse the debate, because the thesis of his opponent is incomplete, and discussion would lead to nothing but empty wrangling.

One frequent cause of dispute amongst philosophers is the question what *things* really are. The representative of a Positivistic school asserts : " A thing is a complex of sense-data ; " his Realistic adversary replies : " No, a thing is a complex of physical matter ; " and an endless and futile argument is thus begun. Yet both are right after all ; the controversy has arisen only on account of the unfortunate use of the material mode.

Let us translate the two theses into the formal mode. That of the Positivist becomes : " Every sentence containing a thing-designation is equipollent with a class of sentences which contain no thing-designations, but sense-data-designations," which is true ; the transformation into sense-data-sentences has often been shown in epistemology. That of the Realist takes the form : " Every sentence containing a thing-designation is equipollent with a sentence containing no thing-designation, but space-time-co-ordinates and physical functions," which is obviously also true.

In this case we do not even need to refer

to two different language-systems in order to make the two theses compatible with one another. They are right in relation to our general language. Each of them asserts the possibility of a certain transformation of thing-sentences. As both kinds of transformation are found feasible, there is no inconsistency. In the original formulation in the material mode the theses *seemed* to be incompatible, because they *seemed* to concern the essence of things, both of them having the form: "A thing is such and such."

5. *Epistemology.*

So far we have considered several examples of philosophical questions, and we have seen that we can translate these questions from the commonly used material mode of speech into the formal mode. By the possibility of this translation it is shown that they belong to syntax. Now the question arises whether the same consideration likewise applies to all other problems and theses of philosophy (where ' philosophy,' as explained before, is understood to include neither metaphysics nor psychology). It is my contention that it does. Let us glance at the principal parts of philosophy in order to examine this assertion.

Epistemology or theory of knowledge in its usual form contains both psychological and logical questions. The psychological questions here concern the procedure of knowledge, that is, the mental events by which we come to know something. If we surrender these questions to the psychologist for his empirical investigation, there remains the logical analysis of knowledge, or more precisely, the logical analysis of the examination and verification of assertions, because knowledge consists of positively verified assertions. Epistemological questions of this kind can certainly be expressed in the formal mode, because epistemological analysis, the question of the verification of a given sentence, has to refer—as we found in the first chapter— to those observation sentences which are deducible from the sentence in question. Thus the logical analysis of verification is the *syntactical* analysis of those transformation rules which determine the deduction of observation sentences. Hence *epistemology* — after elimination of its metaphysical and psychological elements —*is a part of syntax.*

6. *Natural Philosophy*.

It may seem, perhaps, more important to give our attention to some of the special divisions of philosophy, than to discuss the general questions of epistemology. What is called *Natural Philosophy* is, in particular, attracting more and more interest at the present time. What is the subject-matter of this part of philosophy? Is its task the philosophical investigation of nature? The answer is, No; there can be no such thing as a philosophical investigation of nature, because whatever can be said about nature, that is about any events in time and space and about their connections, has to be said by the scientist on the basis of empirical investigation. There remains nothing for the philosopher to say in this field. Metaphysicians do, indeed, venture to make a lot of statements about nature, but such metaphysics is, as we have seen, not theory, but rather poetry. The object of scientifically treated natural philosophy is not nature, but the natural sciences, and its task is the logical analysis of science, in other words, the *syntactical* analysis of the language-system of science.

If in natural philosophy we deal, for instance, with the structure of space and time, then we are occupied in fact with the syntactical analysis of the rules which determine the formation or transformation of space- and time-expressions. The point may be clarified by considering the following thesis, which asserts one of the principal features of the space-time-structure : " Time is one-dimensional ; space is three-dimensional." This sentence can be translated into the formal mode as follows : " A time-designation consists of one co-ordinate ; a space-designation consists of three co-ordinates." In the same way the sentence " Time is infinite in both directions, namely that of the past and that of the future," can be translated into the sentence : " Any real-number-expression, positive or negative, without limit, can be taken as a time-co-ordinate." The question : " Has space a Euclidean or a non-Euclidean structure?" becomes, in the formal mode : " Are the syntactical rules according to which from certain distances others can be calculated, of the Euclidean type or of one of the non-Euclidean types ? "

Thus all questions about the structure of space and time are *syntactical* questions, that is, questions about the structure of the language, and especially the structure of the formation and transformation rules concerning space- and time-co-ordinates.

In addition to the problems of space and time, contemporary natural philosophy is especially concerned with the problems of *causality*. These problems are syntactical problems concerning the syntactical structure of the system of physical laws, as for instance the question whether fundamental physical laws have the type of deterministic laws or that of merely statistical laws. This logical question is the core of the whole problem of Determinism, which is nearly always expressed in the material mode, and is in addition often mixed up with metaphysical pseudo-problems. Consequently its character as a syntactical problem has not been recognized.

The objection may perhaps be raised at this point that the form of physical laws depends upon the experimental results of physical investigations, and that it is not determined by a merely theoretical syntactical consideration. This assertion is quite right, but we must bear in mind the fact that the empirical results at which physicists arrive by way of their laboratory experiments by no means *dictate their choice* between the deterministic and the statistical form of laws. The form in which a law is to be stated has to be decided by an act of volition. This decision, it is true, depends upon the empirical results, but not logically, only practically. The results of the experiments show merely that one mode of formulation would be more suitable than another, that is, more suitable with regard to the whole system of physics. However close the practical connection between the empirical results and the form of physical laws may be, the question concerning the form of these laws is in every case a syntactical question, that is, a question which has to be formulated in syntactical terms.

It is, to be sure, a syntactical question concerning a language-system which has not yet been stated, but is still a matter of discussion. And in this discussion about the future form of physical language and especially the form of fundamental physical laws, physicists as well as logicians have to take part. A satisfactory solution can only be found if both points of view, the empirical view of physics and the formal one of syntax, are taken into consideration. This applies not only to the special problem of causality and determinism, but generally to all problems of natural philosophy, to all questions of the logical analysis of empirical science. All such questions are *syntactical* problems, but in their treatment the results of *empirical* investigation have also to be taken into consideration.

7. *What Physicalism Asserts.*

As there is no philosophy of nature, but only a philosophy of natural science, so there is no special philosophy of life or philosophy of the organic world, but only a philosophy of biology; no philosophy of mind, or philosophy of the psychic world, but only a philosophy of psychology; and finally, no philosophy of history or philosophy of society, but only a philosophy of historical and social sciences; always remembering that the philosophy of a science is the syntactical analysis of the language of that science.

The principal problems concerning such a language of a certain region of science are the questions as to the character of the terms contained therein, the character of the sentences, and above all the transformation or translation rules connecting that language with the other special languages, that is, with the other part-systems of the whole language of science. Of these languages the physical, or that in which we speak about physical things in every-day life or in physics, is of the greatest importance. In our discussions in the *Vienna Circle* we have arrived at the opinion that this physical language is the basic language of all science, that it is a universal language comprehending the contents of all other scientific languages. In other words, every sentence of any branch of scientific language is equipollent to some sentence of the physical language, and can therefore be translated into the physical language without changing its content. Dr. *Neurath*, who has greatly stimulated the considerations which lead to this thesis, has proposed to call it the thesis of *physicalism*.

For purposes of elucidation, let us take the following psychological statement : " At ten o'clock Mr. A was angry." The equipollent sentence of the physical language is : " At ten o'clock Mr. A was in a certain bodily condition which is characterized by the acceleration of breathing and pulsation, by the tension of certain muscles, by the tendency to certain violent behaviour, and so on." Let us express the quality of being angry by the symbol ' Q_1,' the above described physical quality of a body by ' Q_2,' and the time of ten o'clock by ' t_1.' Then we may write the two sentences symbolically in the following way :

(Psychological) $Q_1(A, t_1)$ (S_1)

(Physical) $Q_2(A, t_1)$ (S_2)

Now there is a scientific law, that is, a universal sentence belonging to the valid sentences of the scientific language-system, which says that whenever someone is angry his body is in the physical condition described, and *vice versa*. This is expressed in symbols by :

$$(x) \ (t) \ [Q_1 \ (x, \ t) \equiv Q_2 \ (x, \ t)]$$

(The sign of equivalence ' $\equiv$ ' expresses the implication in both directions.) We have supposed that the quality Q_2 is chosen in such a way that this law is a valid scientific law, that is, either itself a transformation rule or deducible by the help of such rules. It need not be analytic ;

the only assumption is that it is valid. It may be synthetic, in which case it is P-valid. It is obvious that the sentence S_2 can be deduced from S_1 by the help of this law ; and likewise S_1 from S_2. Thus S_1 and S_2 are mutual consequences and hence equipollent. (It is to be remarked that they may be P-consequences and therefore P-equipollent ; in the former explanations of physicalism this possibility is not taken sufficiently into account.)

The question may perhaps be raised whether we really can be sure that for any psychological quality Q_1 there is to be found a corresponding physical quality Q_2 of such a kind that the general equivalence can be stated as valid. If there were a quality Q_1 without such a corresponding quality Q_2, then the psychological sentence '$Q_1(A, t_1)$' could not be translated into the physical language, and the thesis of physicalism would be disproved.

My answer is that there cannot be such an untranslatable quality-sign or predicate in the psychological language. For if in this language there is a predicate 'Q_1' with a meaning, then the sentence '$Q_1(A, t_1)$' must be empirically examinable ; the psychologist must be able to

recognize under suitable circumstances
whether the person A is in the condition
Q_1 or not. But this recognition depends
upon the observable physical behaviour
of A ; hence there is a corresponding
physical quality Q_2, to which this behaviour is linked.

It will no doubt be objected that
there is conceivable a psychological quality Q_1 which never has any effect upon
behaviour ; although feelings like anger
or pleasure are for the most part
expressed in an easily observable manner, there might be other mental
states, such perhaps as thinking, which
never had external consequences. Let us
suppose that there is a kind of mental
state without external consequences, and
that the predicate 'Q_1' is chosen to
designate such a state in psychological language. By what means can the psychologist assert that a person A is in the state
Q_1, if there is not the least effect of this
state to be observed ? To this it will
perhaps be answered that though it may
be impossible for the psychologist to
recognize such a state in another person,
nevertheless the predicate 'Q_1' can be
used by him in describing his own mental

state, because for the recognition of that he does not need any external manifestation ; he recognizes his state directly by introspection, and then uses the predicate ' Q_1 ' to express his findings, in the form, for instance, ' Q_1 (I, now).' Granting that such an extreme case is possible, it does not affect the argument ; for if events take the course supposed, then there still *is* an observable expression of the mental state, namely, the written or spoken assertion of the psychologist.

If, as under suitable conditions we may do, we believe him, that is, accept his statement as a sufficient symptom of his really being in the state asserted, we may ourselves assert that he is now in that state, that is, we may assert the sentence ' Q_1 (P, now) '—' P ' being the name of the psychologist. But such a statement is only the expression in psychological language of the physical statement ' Q_2 (P, now) ' where Q_2 is the physical state of the body of P which we infer from our observation of the physical act by which P communicates the results of his introspection.

We may sum up the results of our investigation as follows. Firstly : If there is in the psychological language a predicate which is originally used only in describing one's *own* mental state, experienced by introspection, then the mere using of this predicate in speaking or writing *is* in fact an expression of that state. Thus the psychological language can contain no predicate which designates a kind of state for which no expression exists. Secondly: Even a predicate which is originally used only in regard to the speaker himself on the basis of his introspection, can subsequently be used also by one person in regard to another, on the basis of the linguistic expressions of the latter, even if no other than *linguistic* expressions of the state designated by the predicate exist. So much may be said in reply to one of the strongest objections to physicalism.

8. *What Physicalism Does Not Assert.*

Now let me say a little more about what the thesis of physicalism really asserts. For objections to this thesis give less trouble to its proponents than misunderstandings of its meaning. In order to make the thesis of physicalism as comprehensible as possible, I might be tempted to formulate it as follows : To every psychical state there is a corresponding physical state of the body, the latter connected with the former by universal laws ; and therefore to every psychological sentence, say S_1, there is a corresponding physical sentence, say S_2, so that S_1 and S_2 are equipollent on account of certain valid laws. But only the second half of this formulation, namely that half concerning the sentences S_1 and S_2, is correct. The first half, referring to psychical and physical states, belongs to the material mode of speech and may easily lead us to pseudo-questions.

For instance, if I speak about the psychical state described by the sentence S_1 and the physical state described by S_2, we may be tempted to raise the question whether they are really two states or only one and the same state regarded from two different points of view ; and further, if they are two states, we may ask what relation there is between them to explain their simultaneous occurrence, and in particular whether this relation is the relation of causality or that of mere parallelism. Thus we shall find ourselves

sliding into the midst of metaphysics—
and that is sliding into the mud.

The questions mentioned belong, indeed,
to one of the most famous philosophical
problems, the so-called psycho-physical
problem. Nevertheless they are pseudo-
questions, they have no theoretical sense.
All the questions that have sense in this
connection can be formulated in the formal
mode, that is by referring to sentences.
It is characteristic of the above metaphysical questions that they can only be
expressed in the material mode, by referring to states, not to sentences.

Among the formal questions which really
have sense, perhaps the most important in
this connection is whether or not to every
psychological sentence S_1 there is a corresponding physical sentence S_2 which is
equipollent with S_1. The thesis of
physicalism answers this question in the
affirmative, but this position is, of course,
always open to discussion if objections
are brought against it. The question of
physicalism is a scientific, and more precisely, a logical, a syntactical, question ;
it can only be settled by further consideration and debate. But whether, using
the material mode, one should speak about

two different states, a psychical and a physical state, or about only one, is merely a question of the determination of the use of language, a question of taste, so to speak. It is by no means a question of fact, as metaphysicians in their controversies believe:

9. *The Unity of Science.*

In close connection with physicalism is the thesis of the *unity of science*. If every sentence can be translated into the physical language, then this language is an all-embracing language, a universal language of science. The existence of one language-system in which every scientific term is contained, however, implies that all these terms are of logically related kinds, and that there cannot be a fundamental division between the terms of the different branches of science. Physical sciences, psychology, social sciences, may indeed for practical purposes be separated, because one scientist cannot deal with all subjects ; but they stand on the same basis, they constitute, in the last analysis, one uniform science.

Should anyone ask me whether that means that all objects in all branches of science are of the same kind, I might answer in the affirmative. But it is to be noted that both the question and the answer belong to the material mode, and I hope that no one who has read so far will be sufficiently unwary of its pitfalls to interpret my reply as an acceptance of the metaphysical thesis of monism. Physicalism and the thesis of the unity of language and of science have nothing to do with any such theses as monism, dualism, or pluralism. My reference to the uniformity of objects was only a concession to the usual mode of speech. To speak correctly, I must speak not about objects but about terms, and my statement becomes : the terms of all branches of science are logically uniform.

It was not my aim here to convince anyone of the truth of our theses of physicalism and the unity of science. I have only tried to make them clear, and especially to show that they are not in any way metaphysical theses concerning the essence of things, but only logical, which is to say syntactical theses. The explanation of physicalism was merely a special example of what I had previously said in general : namely, that all theses and questions of logical analysis and therefore all theses and questions of philosophy (in our sense of this word) belong to logical syntax. The method of logical syntax, that is, the analysis of the formal structure of language as a system of rules, is the only method of philosophy.

LITERATURE.

1. *Rejection of Metaphysics*, on the basis of an analysis of language :

L. Wittgenstein, *Tractatus Logico-Philosophicus*. With an Introduction by B. Russell. London 1922.

C. K. Ogden and I. A. Richards, *The Meaning of Meaning*. A study of the Influence of Language upon Thought and of the Science of Symbolism. London (1923), 3rd ed. 1930.

R. Carnap, *Ueberwindung der Metaphysik durch logische Analyse der Sprache*. Erkenntnis 2, 1931. (French Translation : *La Science et la Metaphysique*. Actualités Scientifiques, vol. 172, Paris 1934.)

2. *Logical Syntax*, and its relation to philosophy:

R. Carnap, *Logische Syntax der Sprache*. (Schriften zur wiss. Weltauffassung, Bd. 8) Wien 1934. An English translation will be published in the *Psyche Monograph* series in 1935.

3. *Physicalism :*

O. Neurath, *Physicalism*. The Philosophy of the Viennese Circle. Monist 41, 1931.

O. Neurath, *Physikalismus*. Scientia 50, 1931.

O. Neurath, *Soziologie im Physikalismus*. Erkenntnis 2, 1931.

O. Neurath, *Einheitswissenschaft und Psychologie*. (Einheitswiss., Heft 1) Wien 1933.

R. Carnap, *The Unity of Science*. With an Introduction by M. Black. (Psyche-Miniatures) London 1934. (Translation of : *Die physikalische Sprache als Universalsprache der Wissenschaft*, Erkenntnis 2, 1931).

R. Carnap, *Psychologie in physikalischer Sprache*. Erkenntnis 3, 1932.

100